The Franz Anton Mesmer Show

David Barry

Beercott

The Franz Anton Mesmer Show
A play in 2 acts

First Published in Great Britain in 2019 by Beercott Books.

ISBN: 978-1-9997429-7-3

David Barry has asserted his rights to be identified
as the author of this book.

A catalogue record of this book is available from the British Library.

Worldwide licence enquiries for this title should be directed to:
licensing@beercottbooks.co.uk.
Title subject to availability.

www.beercottbooks.co.uk

Beercott

An actor's view of the play...

David Barry takes us into a rehearsal room where a late run through of a play concerning the life of Franz Mesmer is about to begin. As the fascinating story of Mesmer's life unfolds, moving between the Imperial Court of Vienna and Revolutionary Paris, the frequently strained and often combustible relations between the cast begin to unravel and the interplay between epic narrative and thespian skirmishing proves truly mesmerising.

Hugh Fraser, actor & crime writer (Captain Hastings in television's *Poirot*)

David Barry has used his insight and understanding of his subject to bring to life both the back stage drama of bringing a play to the stage, with all the problems a production throws at the creative team? Plus the egos, sensibilities and massaging of its cast, coupled with the history of a science I have long studied and practised, he gives us an insight into one of its founders. A subject many are frightened of, but more fascinated by?

Graham Cole OBE, actor (P.C. Tony Stamp in *The Bill*)

Within the confines of the rehearsal room, as the actors prepare a play, their own lives, trials and tribulations become entwined and are laid bare. A cleverly constructed play from David Barry, where life is imitating art.

Linda Marlowe, actor (Sylvie Carter in *EastEnders*)

The story centres around a group of actors rehearsing for a production of a play about the Life of Franz Mesmer, a Viennese healer. It is a play within a play, but Barry makes it very clear which character, or actor, is speaking.
Written by an actor, one can be confident it gives first-hand knowledge of the relationships and often clashes of personalities, artistic thoughts, and patience that an actor goes through from the rehearsal room to the performance. Also a fascinating insight into Franz Mesmer's life and times. Great fun.

Linda Regan, actor & crime writer (April in BBC's *Hi-Di-Hi*)

About the Author

David Barry, was born and bred in North Wales, and has been an actor for more than 50 years. He began working professionally at the age of 12, and a highlight of his early years was touring Europe with Laurence Olivier and Vivien Leigh in Titus Andronicus. He also appeared on the West End stage with Paul Scofield in Graham Greene's The Power and the Glory. In his early twenties he played Frankie Abbott in the successful television sitcom Please Sir! and the film of the same name.

When he appeared in a spin-off of the series, The Fenn Street Gang, he wrote one of the episodes which was accepted by LWT and broadcast. In the mid-70s he co-wrote the sketch show The Lads from Fenn Street, in which he also toured nationally for 18 weeks with two of his Fenn Street colleagues. Then in 1980, having appeared as Elvis, Stratford Johns' nephew, in George and Mildred – the Movie, he wrote three episodes for Thames Television's Keep It in The Family.

David always wanted to write novels, and after two failed attempts, his first novel Each Man Kills was published in 2002, followed by an American crime novel based on a true story, Willie the Actor, published three years later. In 2008 he spent a year in Aberdeen working as a Writer in Residence with children, during which time he completed a children's book, The Ice Cream Time Machine.

Since then he has written several crime novels, including Muscle and A Deadly Diversion. He also wrote the historical novel Mr Micawber Down Under which he later adapted into a play which toured south east England. In 2016, he reintroduced his Abbott character in a play A Day in The Lives of Frankie Abbott, set in a care home, which played at Edinburgh Fringe Festival and received a 5-star review. His one act-play, A Friend of Ronnie's, also toured as a double bill, and in the autumn 2018 played for 12 performances by Newquay Dramatic Society. His latest crime novel, Walking Shadows is due for publication in 2019.

David also presents a weekly radio show on the digital station Channel Radio, a live show which broadcasts every Saturday lunchtime, a show in which he has had many great guests, including Tom Baker, Brian Murphy, Glen Gregory of Heaven 17, Linda Marlowe and many others.

Because of his early years as a child actor, during which his entire education consisted of appearing in plays by Shakespeare, Wilde and Shaw, and dozens of others, he has himself become an obsessional writer, and storytelling is in his blood. He lives in Tunbridge Wells, and has two grown up children.

The Franz Anton Mesmer Show

CHARACTERS

HARRY (40s)

GORDON (Late 50s)

HEATHER (30s)

EMMA (20s)

SANDY (Early 50s)

CARL (40s)

DARYL (Late 20s)

ACT ONE

A rehearsal space; or the setting could be a bare theatre stage set for a rehearsal. There are two tables next to each other, one has papers and a laptop on it – this is the writer's table - and the other has papers, a script and a CD player – this is the director's table. There are chairs at the side of the stage and there is another table for props and rehearsal costumes.

It is early September and the actors wear light summer clothes, so that their rehearsal costumes can easily be worn on top.

Sitting behind the director's table is HEATHER, busy trying to learn lines from a script. She sighs impatiently and looks at her watch.

Sitting the other side of the stage are DARYL and EMMA, DARYL sipping coffee from a Starbucks (or similar) carton.

HARRY enters hurriedly, followed by CARL and SANDY, all carrying cartons of coffee. HARRY has two cartons of coffee, one of which he gives to HEATHER

HARRY: There you go – one latte.

HEATHER: Thanks, Harry. How much do I owe you?

HARRY: Have that one on me. *(She goes to object and he raises a hand.)* No arguments.

HEATHER: Thanks. Any sign of Gordon while you were out?

HARRY shakes his head.

HEATHER: Anyone tried his mobile?

SANDY: I did. He said he was just parking the car. *(Looking at her watch.)* But that was at least fifteen minutes ago.

DARYL: Maybe he had to move it again.

CARL: I think we ought to make a start. I mean, Gordon's not in the first scene.

HEATHER: But what about the warm-up?

CARL: Oh, sod the warm-up. Let's get on with it. We open next Thursday – less than a week away – and still you want us to play games.

HEATHER: Games!

CARL: Yes, when we agreed to mount a devised piece of theatre – with our illustrious writer *(acknowledging HARRY)* - I didn't think we would spend a whole week playing games.

HEATHER *(Coldly)*: They were improvisations, helping us to work together as a team...

EMMA: I thought the first week was fun.

HEATHER: Thank you, Emma.

CARL: But a whole week. It's put us behind. And then we lost Siobhan.

HEATHER: But we didn't know we were going to lose her, did we?

DARYL: Three episodes of *EastEnders*. How bad is that?

HEATHER: Six lines in a soap? How *challenging* is that?

EMMA: But you never know. They might like her character and keep her on.

CARL: Unlikely. She dies in her third episode. So unless they bring her back as a ghost...

EMMA *(Giggling)*: Well, you never know. Stranger things have happened.

HARRY: And I didn't envisage becoming involved as an actor.

HEATHER: It's only a few small scenes, Harry. You'll be fine

GORDON enters, full of apologies and large gestures of remorse.

GORDON: Morning, everyone. So, so sorry. The traffic was unbloodybelievable. I do apologise. The only thing that kept me from having a coronary due to stress was the realisation that I'm not in the first scene.

SANDY: Fifteen minutes ago you said you were parking the car. Where the hell have you parked? John O'Groats?

GORDON: Some woman recognised me from years ago. Wanted my autograph.

DARYL: And it took you fifteen minutes to write your name?

GORDON: She wanted to talk about the old programme. One of her favourite telly series she said. Nostalgia, you see.

SANDY: So you found it difficult to resist talking about yourself again.

GORDON stares at her frostily.

GORDON: I found it difficult to ignore her. It would have been rude. And, like I said, it's not as if I'm in the first scene.

CARL: But Heather was waiting to start with a warm-up.

GORDON *(Huge astonishment)*: I thought we'd gone beyond that stage.

CARL: That's what I said.

HEATHER: Five minutes is all I ask. Just five minutes to get us in the mood.

GORDON: Sorry, love, to disagree. But my warm-up starts with *The Times* crossword. Give us a nudge when you reach scene two.

GORDON goes and sits down, gets his paper out of his bag and starts on the crossword. HEATHER is seething.

HEATHER: I need the warm-up as much as the rest of you. Especially me, since I've been forced to take over Siobhan's roles – in order to save the show. So I think the least you can do is give me some support. You all agreed months back that I would hold workshops, improvisations and direct this devised drama. I never thought I'd have to perform as well.

CARL: Well, I suppose five minutes won't do any harm.

SANDY *(Glaring pointedly at GORDON)*: Might even do us some good.

They all get ready for the warm-up, with the exception of GORDON who remains seated, and also HARRY who is typing away on his laptop.

HEATHER: Physical warm-up. Walk like the character you are playing. Stop and confront each other physically.

EMMA: But I'm playing loads of characters.

SANDY: We all are.

HEATHER: Choose any one of them. We should be able to tell who you are by your demeanour, the way you walk, and they way you approach someone physically. Now go! Start milling about.

They all start walking about and improvising characters' walks. GORDON snorts disgustedly.

GORDON: We did this on day two of our rehearsal four weeks ago. A whole bloody hour we spent on it. Looking like lost souls at Stansted Airport after their flights have been cancelled.

HEATHER *(Patiently)*: Oh come on, Gordon. Just walk about for a bit as Mesmer.

GORDON: I've come to the conclusion, Heather, that Mesmer walks pretty much like Gordon walks. *(Focusing on the crossword.)* Thirteen down. Eleven letters. "Crenelation reconstructed for historical epic."

There is some more milling about, with HEATHER deeply into her character now, twisting and turning like an old witch.

HARRY: I'm still not happy with the way Mesmer is introduced. The audience should know more about his early life. And why not much was known about his relationship with a wife ten years older than him, and a stepson he was devoted to.

HEATHER: Just give us a moment, Harry. We can discuss this when we finish the warm-up.

EMMA: I've guessed which character you are, Heather.

SANDY: She's not the Empress, that's for sure.

EMMA: I think the mother is a frightening old witch. Definitely had a screw loose.

HEATHER *(Staring pointedly at CARL)*: Obviously you're not the father, Carl.

CARL: I thought I'd do Robespierre in Act Two.

HEATHER: I was hoping you might give us the father with some dramatic movement. He was clearly a monster, requiring strong physical commitment.

GORDON *(Peering over his paper)*: With all due respect, Heather, we need the audience to believe these characters, otherwise it could degenerate into pantomime.

HEATHER *(Heatedly)*: Pantomime has to be as real and as believable as any other genre. Just larger than life, that's all.

GORDON: Oh. So you admit we're going down the panto route.

HEATHER *(Passionately)*: If it means the audience are going to be entertained and stimulated, and leave the theatre moved by the story of the man who was the father of hypnosis, then I don't see anything wrong in adopting a panto style.

HARRY: But Mesmer deserves more respect than a…a variety show about him. It's turning out like a series of sketches about the Hapsburg Empire.

DARYL: Not to mention the French Revolution.

HEATHER *(To HARRY)*: But it seems to be working, Harry.

HARRY: Playing around with history.

HEATHER: The audience don't want a history lesson.

HARRY: Nor do they want to be fooled into believing in a load of events which were untrue.

HEATHER: We haven't been inaccurate – you've made sure of that with your research – we've just changed the timing of certain events.

EMMA: Well, I think it's a fun show. And at least I know a little about Mesmer now. I'd never heard of him before.

SANDY: And most of the audiences won't either.

HARRY *(Gradually coming round)*: Well, I suppose…it's just I hadn't thought of the piece going in the pop theatre direction. I mean, adopting a Joan Littlewood style's all very well…

HEATHER: Look at how successful *Oh What a Lovely War* was – and still is from time to time. If we can do the same with Mesmer…

HARRY: Her swan song was *Twang!* A musical about Robin Hood. People walked out in droves. And that was just the cast.

CARL: Ah, but that was mainly Lionel Bart's fault. Littlewood walked out long before the first night, unable to cope with his alcoholism and drug taking.

SANDY: Anyway, does it really matter if we change a few things? They do it all the time in the cinema.

DARYL: That's right. What about that Daniel Day Lewis film, *In the Name of the Father*? A true story about a man accused of planting an IRA bomb. His father went to prison, and there was a scene where they met up. Didn't happen, apparently. So who cares?

HEATHER has had enough of the discussion and checks her watch.

HEATHER: God! Look at the time. Let's make a start and see if we can run Act One. I think I'm on top of the lines by now but…Harry, if you could be a sweetie…

HARRY: Sure. I'll go on the book.

GORDON *(To EMMA)*: Judging by your Maria Theresa walk, Emma, I think you've nailed the character. Spot on.

EMMA: Thank you, Gordon.

This intimacy, a moment between EMMA and GORDON, is not lost on SANDY.

HEATHER: And if we could have a bit of music to create the mood. You know how to work it?

HARRY: Er – yes. I think I press 'Play' to play.

They get into their makeshift rehearsal costumes. SANDY, HEATHER and EMMA tie hoops that go beneath crinolines round their waists, and GORDON, CARL and DARYL put on frock coats.

DARYL *(To GORDON)*: I think it was Gatwick not Stansted.

GORDON: Sorry?

DARYL: You know: the cancelled flights.

DARYL mimes the milling about in character.

GORDON *(Not the least bit amused)*: Oh, yes. Very funny, Daryl.

They take their positions for the opening scene, except GORDON and DARYL who sit down again. GORDON takes up the crossword and buries his head in it.

HEATHER cues HARRY for the music, which will be Mozart. HEATHER sweeps on as the EMPRESS, followed by EMMA as 1st LADY-IN-WAITING and SANDY as 2nd LADY-IN-WAITING. The music is blasting out as HEATHER starts to speak. She stops and catches HARRY'S eye, miming for him to fade the music out, which he does.

HEATHER/EMPRESS: Where is my private secretary?

EMMA/1st LADY: You sent him to speak to Salieri, Your Majesty, about the requiem for your dear departed husband.

HEATHER/EMPRESS: Salieri must wait. I have more pressing business concerning my godchild and namesake, Maria Theresa. Fetch Herr Paradies at once.

EMMA/1st LADY: Yes, Your Majesty. *(She exits.)*

HEATHER/EMPRESS *(To the 2nd Lady)*: Tell me, my dear, what do you know of Franz Anton Mesmer?

SANDY/2nd LADY: Dr Mesmer is the talk of Vienna.

HEATHER/EMPRESS *(Impatiently)*: Yes, that much I know.

SANDY/2nd LADY: They call him the Wizard of Vienna.

HEATHER/EMPRESS: Wizard!

SANDY/2nd LADY: They say he is a sorcerer; a magician. But one who can cure the sick where others have failed.

HEATHER/EMPRESS: Well, the others have failed to cure Maria Theresa. We have no choice. We must give Dr Mesmer a chance.

CARL enters as HERR PARADIES with EMMA as 1st LADY who returns to the EMPRESS'S side.

CARL/PARADIES: You wish to see me, Your Majesty.

HEATHER/EMPRESS: It's about your daughter.

CARL/PARADIES: Ah yes: young Mozart wrote her a beautiful composition. I hope you found her recital satisfactory.

HEATHER/EMPRESS: It far exceeded satisfactory. No. What I wish to discuss with you is her affliction. We have done everything to restore her sight.

CARL/PARADIES: Your Majesty has been most generous. She has been treated by every eminent physician in Austria. Alas…

HEATHER/EMPRESS: There is one other. Admittedly a last resort, but we must do everything in our power to assist Maria to overcome her disorder.

CARL/PARADIES: If Your Majesty is referring to the notorious Dr Mesmer…

HEATHER/EMPRESS: Notorious! Surely not.

CARL/PARADIES: There are many rumours circulating about his behaviour. Of course, I'm not one to listen to gossip but –

HEATHER/EMPRESS: But?

CARL/PARADIES: They say he magnetizes the fountains in his garden.

HEATHER/EMPRESS: Whatever else the rumour-mongers may say, he is a scientist, with an excellent training and background in medicine. Magnetizing fountains may seem unconventional to a layperson, but no scientist ever achieved favourable results without experimenting.

CARL/PARADIES: It isn't just the fountains, Your Majesty. I have also heard that he believes animals can foresee the future.

HEATHER/EMPRESS: But he moves in fashionable circles.

CARL/PARADIES: I have heard he dabbles in the black arts. The occult.

HEATHER/EMPRESS: It sounds like tittle-tattle.

CARL/PARADIES: No smoke without fire.

HEATHER/EMPRESS: But Mozart informs me that he treated his wife's cousin for all manner of maladies: convulsions, agonizing headaches, trances, paralysis lasting for days on end. And so effective was her cure, she is now married and has two children. *And* he has treated my daughter Marie Antoinette.

CARL/PARADIES: I had no idea your daughter was afflicted in any way.

HEATHER/EMPRESS: Hot flushes and headaches. Nothing extreme.

CARL/PARADIES: And did this…er…physician cure her?

HEATHER/EMPRESS: She visits him regularly. It gives her a feeling of well-being.

CARL/PARADIES: Hmm. I'm still not convinced.

HEATHER/EMPRESS *(Impatiently)*: Herr Paradies, anyone would think you don't want to find a cure for your daughter.

CARL/PARADIES: That's absurd. *(Realising he has gone too far.)* I beg Your Majesty's pardon.

HEATHER/EMPRESS: Just what is it you have against this man Mesmer? Other than what you hear in the salons and coffee houses.

CARL/PARADIES *(Reluctantly)*: I suppose I have mistakenly listened to idle talk and banter. I will make an effort to judge him with an open mind. *(Aside.)* Even if he is a sorcerer.

HEATHER/EMPRESS: That's settled then...you must take Maria to see him...and the sooner the better.

PARADIES gives the EMPRESS a small bow of acquiescence. She exits followed by her ladies-in-waiting.

CARL/PARADIES: I'm the child's father and I have no choice in the matter. No wonder I'm going to hate you, Dr Mesmer. Oh how I'm going to hate you.

HEATHER: Good, Carl; excellent. Scene two, Gordon. Daryl. Mesmer's home...

GORDON starts to take his position with DARYL, who carries a carpet bag, but HARRY interrupts the start of the scene.

HARRY: Heather, before we move on, can we cut a line?

HEATHER: Which line is that?

HARRY: The one about Paradies hating Mesmer. The last one.

HEATHER: But that's a good ending to the scene, Harry. It needs a suspenseful end, preparing the audience for the trouble ahead.

HARRY: It's just that at first Paradies was far from reluctant to have his daughter treated by Mesmer. He even offered to give him a glowing reference.

HEATHER: But we've already discussed the weirdness of this man and his wife. When they first approach Mesmer, and are supportive of his methods, the audience will see them for the hypocrites they are.

CARL: Yes, I agree with Heather, Harry. The tag of the scene needs to show us how this man is out to cause trouble.

HARRY: Well...all right. But let's see how it pans out with the later scenes. We don't have to decide categorically.

The way the others look at him, he can tell they have already decided this scene will stay as it is.

HARRY: Okay. Sorry to interrupt. It was just a thought.

HEATHER: No, good point, Harry. Now let's move on. Music link, perhaps?

HARRY: Yes. Right.

HARRY operates CD player. Mozart. This time he fades it soon after the entrance of the actors.

GORDON/MESMER enters, followed by DARYL/ASSISTANT, carrying a carpet bag.

GORDON: *(Clicking his fingers as if he has just remembered something.)* Intolerance.

HARRY: That's not the line.

HEATHER: It makes no sense, Gordon.

GORDON It's the solution to thirteen down. It just came to me out the blue. Sorry, sorry. Brain's a funny thing. Won't happen again.

SANDY *(Who has heard it all before)*: Oh, God!

HEATHER *(To HARRY)*: Give Gordon the first line.

GORDON: No, that's all right. I know it. Sorry, Daryl. Here we go.

He pats DARYL on the shoulder, composes himself ready for the entrance, gets into character and enters.

GORDON/MESMER: You've studied my 27 propositions in Animal Magnetism, and the influence of the planets on the human body?

DARYL/ASSIST: Yes. But better still, doctor, I've seen the way you gaze into the patient's eyes to effect a cure. Who could possibly doubt you as a healer?

MESMER looks seriously into his assistant's eyes.

GORDON/MESMER: But I want you to understand, I am not a miracle man. I am a scientist. My cures can be explained.

DARYL/ASSIST: At the university they saw how you demonstrated the use of magnets to heal the sick. But they still don't believe it.

GORDON/MESMER: Vienna is full of bigots. How can I convince those clowns that Animal Magnetism works? *(Feeling a pain in his knee.)* Ouch!

DARYL/ASSIST: What's wrong?

GORDON/MESMER: Oh, it's nothing. I banged my knee getting up from the breakfast table this morning, that's all.

Eagerly, the assistant places the bag on the floor, bends down and starts to open it.

GORDON/MESMER: What are you doing?

DARYL/ASSIST: Getting the magnets.

GORDON/MESMER *(Irritated)*: And what exactly do you propose to do with them?

DARYL/ASSIST: Your knee. Affect a cure. I've seen enough of your work now…I think it's time I had a go.

MESMER pulls the assistant to his feet.

GORDON/MESMER: How many more times do I have to tell you: bruising is physical damage to tissue, and if it is organic it cannot be treated by Animal Magnetism. *(He starts to exit, taking the bag with him.)* I'd better deal with this blacksmith who suffers from fits.

DARYL/ASSIST: But you have one of the richest and most fashionable society ladies waiting to see you.

GORDON/MESMER: In other words, the sick are here. I shall overcharge them as usual, so that the humble blacksmith may receive my treatment gratuitously.

DARYL/ASSIST: That's Marie Antionette out there – soon to marry the heir to the French throne. Let the blacksmith wait.

GORDON/MESMER *(Aside)*: The cheek of this upstart physician. *(To the ASSISTANT.)* Do not presume to tell me how to run my surgery.

MESMER exits, leaving the ASSISTANT alone.

DARYL/ASSIST: And what about me? Always at your beck and call, master. You call me your protégé but you treat me like a servant. You get all the glory…but I'm a physician too. Or I will be someday. Then just you wait, Dr Mesmer. *Just you wait!*

Offstage commotion. THE THREE SOCIETY LADIES ENTER.
1st LADY is MARIE ANTIONETTE, played by SANDY, EMMA is
2nd LADY and HEATHER is 3rd.

SANDY/1ST LADY: I simply must see the doctor.

EMMA/2ND LADY: But I was here before you.

HEATHER/3RD LADY: No. I was here before either of you.

SANDY/1ST LADY: But neither of you look very ill. *(To the ASSISTANT.)* Wouldn't you agree, Dr Mesmer?

DARYL/ASSIST: I'm afraid I'm not...

EMMA/2ND LADY *(To 1st LADY)*: You're not exactly at death's door yourself.

SANDY/1ST LADY: No, but I'm plagued with boredom.

HEATHER/3RD LADY *(Almost fainting)*: Oh please don't mention the plague.

SANDY/1ST LADY: So bored. Bored with the opera, bored with society and bored with Vienna.

EMMA/2ND LADY: I know exactly how you feel. At least Dr Mesmer is the latest attraction.

HEATHER/3RD LADY: The very latest fashion.

EMMA/2ND LADY: A temporary respite from ennui. Do you know, I have been to séances, but even they become boring after a while.

SANDY/1st LADY: The last time I was at a séance I had a vision of a woman knitting by the guillotine. *(To the ASSISTANT.)* Now tell us, Doctor: what do we have to do?

DARYL/ASSIST: Well, ladies, you see I'm not...

EMMA/2ND LADY: Princess Belvedere has already been treated by the good doctor. She visits him regularly.

HEATHER/3rd LADY: Oh does she?

EMMA/2nd LADY: Yes, she was hysterical before she came to see him. She used to have two crises a week.

SANDY/1ST LADY: And now?

EMMA/2ND LADY: Now she has two a day.

They all giggle.

DARYL/ASSIST: Perhaps I ought to explain: the crisis precedes the cure.

HEATHER/1ST LADY: Oh good. Then you may start whenever you wish, doctor.

DARYL/ASSIST: Er – that's what I was trying to explain. I am not Dr Mesmer.

SANDY/1ST LADY *(Horrified)*: Not Dr Mesmer?

DARYL/ASSIST: I'm his assistant.

SANDY/1st LADY *(Aside)*: He deceives me! The Empress's daughter.

DARYL/ASSIST: I sincerely regret to inform you that Dr Mesmer is treating another patient.

EMMA/2ND LADY: It must be someone extremely important. Royalty, perhaps?

DARYL/ASSIST: Er – not exactly.

HEATHER/3RD LADY: Then pray tell us who the doctor considers to be of more importance than we three celebrated ladies?

DARYL/ASSIST: A blacksmith.

EMMA/2ND LADY: Oh! How disgusting!

HEATHER/3RD LADY: Humiliating. Let us adjourn to the nearest coffee house. *(Aside.)* To spread malicious rumours.

2nd and 3rd LADY exit.

SANDY/1ST LADY: How can someone from such a low station in life afford such treatment?

DARYL/ASSIST: For the poor there is no charge. And the blacksmith has fallen on hard times. He can't afford to buy bread to feed his family.

SANDY/1ST LADY: Then let them eat cake. *(Aside.)* Oh, I say! That's really rather good. I must use that someday.

She exits.

DARYL/ASSIST: Look out, Dr Mesmer, the tide of good fortune may turn against you.

HEATHER: Scene three. Mesmer's study.

> *GORDON sets his own chair and a small table as a desk. He sits at the desk and begins reading. DARYL prepares to enter, knocks on an imaginary door, enters and then stops.*

HEATHER: What's wrong?

DARYL: Siobhan was originally playing Mesmer's servant. Now I've got to play it. And as I'm playing his assistant the audience won't be able to tell the characters apart.

HEATHER: You'll have a change of costume

DARYL: Giving the impression the *assistant* has dressed differently

HEATHER: So why not play the servant with a dialect of some sort?

> *DARYL thinks about this, and then visibly brightens as he makes up his mind.*

DARYL: Right. I'll give it a go.

> *He turns around, goes to his entrance again and prepares himself. He knocks on the imaginary door and enters.*

DARYL/SERVANT *(German accent)*: Sir! Zerr iss a Herr and Frau Paradies vaiting outside. Zay demand to see you at vonce.

> *Nonplussed, GORDON looks slowly round at DARYL.*

GORDON: You're not serious, are you?

DARYL: What?

GORDON: You sound like a Nazi in *Allo, Allo*. Why the German accent?

DARYL: Austrian, German: what's the difference?

HEATHER: What I meant was, Daryl, try and give him an English regional accent. Cockney or something.

DARYL: Cockney!

GORDON: Yes, dear boy. Unlike the young physician, it makes him more working class, d'you see.

DARYL *(Dawning on him)*: Oh. Right!

He goes through the same routine of entering again.

DARYL/SERVANT: Sir, there's a Herr and Frau Paradies waiting outside. They demand to see you at once.

GORDON is unable to get his next line out as he corpses over DARYL'S Dick Van Dyke cockney.

DARYL *(To HEATHER)*: I find East End accents difficult.

HEATHER: What about West Country?

DARYL *(Trying it out)*: Zir, there's a Herr and Frau Paradies waitin' outside.

This is as bad as the Cockney and DARYL shakes his head.

HEATHER: Where are your parents from, Daryl?

DARYL: Carshalton Beeches.

HEATHER *(As if this explains everything)*: Ah!

DARYL: But Nanny and Grandpa – my dad's parents – live in Leeds. I could do a Yorkshire accent.

HEATHER: Yorkshire it is then.

As DARYL goes through the same routine, GORDON mutters under his breath.

GORDON: Take twenty-six.

DARYL/SERVANT: Sir! There's a Herr and Frau Paradies waiting outside. They demand to see you at once.

HEATHER gives him the thumbs up sign for his Yorkshire dialect and he gains confidence.

GORDON/MESMER: Demand!

DARYL/SERVANT: They are not blessed with humility.

GORDON/MESMER: Send them away. I'm busy.

DARYL/SERVANT: They have their daughter with them. A young blind girl.

MESMER suddenly realises who she is.

GORDON/MESMER *(Aside)*: Paradies! Of course! The daughter's a ward of the Empress. *(To the SERVANT.)* Show them in.

The SERVANT starts to exit but PARADIES (CARL) and his WIFE (HEATHER) burst in. The mother assists MARIA (EMMA). Without a glance at the servant, Paradies hands him his cane.

CARL/PARADIES: Dr Mesmer?

GORDON/MESMER: Yes?

CARL/PARADIES: My name is Paradies. And this is my lady wife.

GORDON/MESMER: If you require medical attention, you should have seen one of my assistants first.

HEATHER/MOTHER: But don't you know who we are?

GORDON/MESMER: Your name is Paradies. Your husband just told me.

HEATHER/MOTHER: I *meant* you must surely have heard of us. My husband has an important position at the Schonbrunn Palace, as Private Secretary to the Empress.

GORDON/MESMER *(Unimpressed)*: How can I be of service to you?

HEATHER/MOTHER *(Aside to PARADIES)*: You see! I told you it never pays to be so self effacing. *(To MESMER.)* We've come about our gifted daughter – Maria Theresa. She's a talented pianist, you know, and she receives a pension from the Empress.

GORDON/MESMER: I have seen some of your performances, Maria. They were sublime.

EMMA/MARIA *(Shyly)*: Thank you.

HEATHER/MOTHER: She's nervous and frightened of physicians, doctor; ever since they bombarded her eyes with hundreds of electric shocks. You can't imagine the pain. Her screams were terrifying.

EMMA/MARIA: Please, Mother! Stop!

CARL/PARADIES: Now, now, Maria. Your mother has to tell the doctor.

MESMER goes to MARIA and speaks gently to her.

GORDON/MESMER: There is no need to distress yourself, Maria. I won't hurt you. I want you to place your complete trust in me. Have you been blind since birth?

EMMA/MARIA: No.

CARL/PARADIES: She was struck blind at the age of three and has not been able to see since then.

GORDON/MESMER: Do you have a memory of this incident, Maria?

EMMA/MARIA: No – I –

HEATHER/MOTHER: She couldn't possibly remember. Otherwise we'd have been the first to know after all these years.

GORDON/MESMER *(Ignoring the PARENTS)*: Maria?

EMMA/MARIA: Sometimes I have this dream…I…

GORDON/MESMER: Yes?

EMMA/MARIA: I can hear screaming. Terrible, blood-curdling sounds…

HEATHER/MOTHER: What nonsense this is. Don't waste the doctor's time. *(To MESMER.)* Even though she's blind, she has a vivid imagination.

GORDON/MESMER: Maria Theresa, I want you to be my patient, but you must place yourself in my hands and trust me implicitly. I think I can cure you. *(To the PARENTS.)* But this treatment will only work if I gain her complete trust. Therefore, I propose that she come and stay in this house.

CARL/PARADIES: I don't think I can give my wholehearted approval.

HEATHER/MOTHER: It's quite out of the question. What about her concerts?

GORDON/MESMER: Which is more important, to have her sight restored or to miss a few concerts? *(An uncomfortable silence.)* If you don't mind, Maria, I'd like to speak to your parents alone. Would you mind waiting in the next room? *(He guides her towards the exit.)* You'll find a chair to the right as you enter. I won't be very long.

MARIA THERESA exits and MESMER returns to the PARENTS.

GORDON/MESMER: Maria Theresa's illness would not appear to be physical but hysterical.

CARL/PARADIES: Meaning what exactly?

GORDON/MESMER: That her blindness is self imposed. Something must have happened to her that had such a traumatic effect, causing her to unconsciously reject life as she saw it and retreat into darkness.

HEATHER/MOTHER: But that's absurd. If anything *had* happened, we would have known about it. No, she can't possibly stay here.

CARL/PARADIES: It isn't just a question of her recitals, you understand –

GORDON/MESMER: What then?

CARL/PARADIES: This house – it has a reputation –

GORDON/MESMER: For curing diseases where others have failed. If you're so opposed to my methods and my "reputation", why did you bring her here?

CARL/PARADIES: It was the Empress's idea.

GORDON/MESMER: I see. Well, you had better do as the Empress suggests, hadn't you? *(Anticipating the mother's objection.)* And please don't worry about Maria's talent. I myself am devoted to music. She will be able to practice every day. So there can be no further objections, can there?

CARL/PARADIES: Well…no…but…

GORDON/MESMER: Now, if you will excuse me, I have a busy day ahead. Have Maria's belongings brought here as soon as possible. My servant will see you out.

MESMER exits.

CARL/PARADIES: What a rude man!

HEATHER/MOTHER: You weakling. You were so easily persuaded.

CARL/PARADIES: I was thinking of Maria.

HEATHER/MOTHER: You were thinking of yourself. Wondering what you could tell the Empress. You're such a worm.

She exits.

CARL/PARADIES *(Calling after her)*: Well…what would you have done in my place?

He exits hurriedly.

HEATHER: Now we go to the composite scene, but Carl and I will enter after the first short scene.

GORDON fetches a prop wand from the prop table, takes a position standing close to EMMA, and starts to wave the wand to the side of her face.

GORDON: Sorry to stop a minute; I'd just like to check something. I'm not convinced by this wand business.

HARRY: It actually happened, Gordon. It's on record. Mesmer believed in the effect of gravitation on human physiology. He believed there was a universal fluid, a magnetism of light and heat, and all things were immersed in this magnetic, cosmic sea, which he thought he could harness to cure his patients.

He was wrong, of course. What he didn't know was that he'd unwittingly discovered hypnosis, and he cured his patients by putting them in a trance.

GORDON: But why the wand?

HARRY: He believed he'd magnetized it with the cosmic fluid, but I suspect it worked much the same way as you see music hall hypnotists dangling a watch in front of someone to put them in a trance.

GORDON: So presumably Maria Theresa can instinctively sense where he has the wand and his voice soothes her into a trance.

HARRY: Exactly!

GORDON: Good. Sorry to hold things up, Heather. I just need to be absolutely clear about this in performance.

HEATHER: No problem, Gordon. It's a learning curve for all of us.

GORDON: Okay. Back to the plot.

He takes up his position with MARIA again, holding the wand close to her face.

GORDON/MESMER: Which side is it?

EMMA/MARIA: On my right.

GORDON/MESMER: And now?

EMMA/MARIA: On the left.

GORDON/MESMER: Excellent! *(He puts the wand behind his back.)* And now?

EMME/MARIA *(Slight panic)*: I don't know.

GORDON/MESMER: It's behind my back.

She relaxes and laughs.

EMMA/MARIA: Now you're playing tricks on me.

GORDON/MESMER: I can't believe how well you're doing.

EMMA/MARIA: And I still can't believe Mama and Papa didn't object to my staying here.

GORDON/MESMER: Their only concern was for their daughter's welfare.

They both freeze and HEATHER and CARL enter as the parents.

HEATHER/MOTHER: I still don't like it.

CARL/PARADIES: At least it's a relief to know she's not going through the agony of bleedings and purges.

HEATHER/MOTHER: That's all very well, but what if she regains her sight.

CARL/PARADIES: We'll still get the pension from the Empress. It's in recognition of her talent.

HEATHER/MOTHER: *And* as compensation for her disability. *(Suddenly vicious)* Oh why did this witch doctor have to ruin everything?

They freeze. The focus is back on MESMER and MARIA.

EMMA/MARIA: My head is spinning; out of control.

GORDON/MESMER: Please don't be frightened, Maria. Your brain is learning to deal with visual perceptions.

EMMA/MARIA: But the shadows are terrifying. Like a strange dream I once had.

GORDON/MESMER: You've lived in a world of darkness for so long, Maria. At first the light will seem strange and uncomfortable.

EMMA/MARIA: The dark shadows I see are evil.

GORDON/MESMER: They are buried deep within your soul, Maria. They are your past. First you must learn to live in the present. Accept the light. Embrace it. Relax and trust me, Maria.

She stares closely into his face for a long while and runs her hands over his features.

EMMA/MARIA: How strange you seem. But I'm glad it's you I see and no one else.

They freeze. A long pause. DARYL is whispering in SANDY'S ear when he realises HEATHER and the rest of the cast are staring at them.

HEATHER: It's you and Sandy, Daryl. The two gossips.

DARYL: Sorry.

They both get up hurriedly and get into position.

SANDY/GOSSIP: What's happened to Mesmer's wife, that's what I'd like to know?

DARYL/GOSSIP: They live apart. Didn't you know?

SANDY/GOSSIP: Ten years his senior. He only married her for wealth and status.

DARYL/GOSSIP: He's a vampire.

SANDY/GOSSIP: A werewolf.

DARYL/GOSSIP: A lunatic.

SANDY/GOSSIP: That poor little blind pianist.

DARYL/GOSSIP: And she's only 18.

SANDY/GOSSIP: And so talented.

DARYL/GOSSIP: He keeps her there.

SANDY/GOSSIP: Against her will.

DARYL/GOSSIP: And I have heard...

He whispers a juicy bit of scandal in SANDY'S ear and they both screech with laughter. A moment later they become serious again.

DARYL/GOSSIP: He should be executed.

SANDY/GOSSIP: And thrown into an unmarked grave!

DARYL/GOSSIP: Sadly, this is the Age of Reason.

They freeze and the focus shifts to the FATHER and MOTHER.

CARL/PARADIES: This has gone on long enough. I want my daughter home.

HEATHER/MOTHER: It may be too late. She is dependent on another man.

CARL/PARADIES: Everyone in Vienna's talking about it. It's a scandal.

HEATHER/MOTHER: Don't say I didn't warn you.

They freeze. Focus on MARIA and MESMER.

EMMA/MARIA: Everything is confusion. This morning, as I practised, I kept hitting the wrong keys. That has never happened to me before.

GORDON/MESMER: Your music will suffer as your sight improves. You will eventually learn to see, rather than feel, the difference in spaces. It will take time to adjust.

EMMA/MARIA: How long?

GORDON/MESMER: I have no idea.

EMMA/MARIA: But what shall I do about Mama and Papa? My playing means so much to them.

GORDON/MESMER: But what does it mean to you?

EMMA/MARIA: My music means the world to me. And yet, now that I have looked at the night sky and seen the countless stars, I seem to be torn between two worlds.

As they exit, GORDON slips his hand onto EMMA'S back, just below the waist and whispers something to her. She giggles. SANDY notices, and glares at GORDON and gives heavy emphasis to her next line which seems to be directed at GORDON rather than MESMER.

SANDY/GOSSIP: I would never trust a man like that.

DARYL/GOSSIP: Those eyes of his.

SANDY/GOSSIP: And now she can't play a note, poor thing.

DARYL/GOSSIP: He's ruined her.

SANDY/GOSSIP: Destroyed her.

DARYL/GOSSIP: She'll never be the same again.

SANDY/GOSSIP: What's more, he drinks.

DARYL/GOSSIP: It's *what* he drinks.

SANDY/GOSSIP: Young virgin's blood.

They gasp with horrified relish and exit. Focus shifts to MOTHER and FATHER.

CARL/PARADIES: I've come to the conclusion that Maria doesn't want her sight restored.

HEATHER/MOTHER: Not if it means she has to sacrifice her talent.

CARL/PARADIES: A gift, bestowed upon her by Almighty God, to recompense the darkness.

HEATHER/MOTHER: She is selling her soul for a little light.

CARL/PARADIES: And what use is a little light in return for a God-given talent?

HEATHER/MOTHER: We must save her from that monster.

CARL/PARADIES: He's ruined our daughter.

HEATHER/MOTHER: He must be destroyed.

They exit. HARRY operates linking music. DARYL, as the assistant from Scene 2, takes centre stage and paces up and down. As the music fades, MESMER enters

GORDON/MESMER: You wanted to see me.

DARYL/ASSIST: I don't know quite how to tell you this –

GORDON/MESMER: Well? *(Long pause.)* Are you waiting for me to make it easier for you? You wish to leave, is that it?

DARYL/ASSIST: Well...yes...I...

GORDON/MESMER: But why?

DARYL/ASSIST: I just couldn't take all the lies and rumours and insults.

GORDON/MESMER: You think that's easy for me?

The ASSISTANT is stuck for words, either from embarrassment or guilt.

GORDON/MESMER: You were my most trusted physician. More than that: my friend.

DARYL/ASSIST: Your shadow.

GORDON/MESMER: Oh so that's it…you want to be top dog!

MARIA THERESA enters.

EMMA/MARIA: Doctor, I…*(Seeing the ASSISTANT, she stops.)* I'm sorry. I didn't mean to interrupt.

GORDON/MESMER: That's all right, Maria. My old friend is just leaving. Permanently. He has been offered another post.

DARYL/ASSIST *(Surprised)*: But how did you know?

GORDON/MESMER: I don't think there is anything further to be said, do you?

Beat as they stare at each other. Then the ASSISTANT exits. During this exit HARRY creeps across to the upstage area, ready to make his entrance with PARADIES and the MOTHER.

GORDON/MESMER: Everything appears to be falling apart. *(He takes MARIA'S hands and looks into her eyes.)* That is why I have to keep reminding myself: I *have* succeeded, Maria. If ever I had doubts that Animal Magnetism worked, those doubts have vanished forever.

There is a commotion offstage. We hear the SERVANT'S voice shouting.

DARYL/SERVANT *(Offstage)*: No! You can't go in there!

PARADIES bursts into the room, followed by the MOTHER and HARRY as the thug.

CARL/PARADIES: Just as I thought: we've disturbed a rather intimate tête-à-tête,

GORDON/MESMER: How dare you burst in here unannounced.

CARL/PARADIES: And how dare you keep our daughter here against her will. *(To the thug.)* Hold him!

The THUG grabs MESMER'S arm in a half-nelson with another arm round his neck.

EMMA/MARIA: Papa! What's happening? What are you doing?

HEATHER/MOTHER: He's a disgusting man. He should be taught a lesson.

HARRY/THUG: He's an evil fiend.

EMMA/MARIA: But he's given me back my sight.

HEATHER/MOTHER: And robbed you of your talent.

EMMA/MARIA: I love him.

HEATHER/MOTHER *(To PARADIES)*: Did you hear that?

PARADIES, mad with jealousy, grabs MARIA and hurls her to the floor.

CARL/PARADIES: You belong to us – not this charlatan! Do you understand?

EMMA/MARIA: No, Papa! Please!

HEATHER/MOTHER *(Grabbing MARIA by the hair)*: Shut up! Shut up! Or I'll really give you something to cry about.

EMMA/MARIA: Why, Mama? Why?

HEATHER/MOTHER: Because you can't play anymore.

CARL/PARADIES: And if you can't play...

HEATHER/MOTHER: You're no good to us.

In her extreme anger, the MOTHER gives MARIA a vicious slap. A long pause. They all watch MARIA as she struggles to her feet

EMMA/MARIA: I can't see. Everything is black again. Pitch black.

PARADIES goes to her side and takes her arm.

CARL/PARADIES: We'll take you home.

HEATHER/MOTHER: Where you belong. You can start practising again.

They start to exit. The THUG pushes MESMER away roughly.

HARRY/THUG: As for you: keep your evil powers to yourself.

The THUG exits, following the MOTHER and MARIA.
PARADIES, who feels he has to justify his actions, turns at the
exit to address MESMER.

CARL/PARADIES: Her sight was never fully restored, you know.

He exits. Beat while MESMER thinks about MARIA and her
monstrous parents. The SERVANT enters, holding his arm as if
it pains him.

DARYL/SERVANT: I'm sorry, sir. I wanted to help, but that
    ruffian had an accomplice. I could do nothing to stop them.

GORDON/MESMER: No one can stop monsters like the Paradies.
    It was they who were responsible for Maria's condition in the
    first place. Oh, she didn't tell me that – not in so many
    words. But something happened when she was only three,
    and I blame those barbarians. They were the ones who
    needed treatment. Not Maria. Poor Maria. Such monsters.

DARYL/SERVANT: At least she has her music, sir.

GORDON/MESMER *(Ironically)*: Ah yes: her music. *(Suddenly*
    shakes himself out of his depression.) How would you like to
    be my valet, my footman and my coachman?

DARYL/SERVANT: Sir?

GORDON/MESMER: It is no longer possible for me to remain in
    Vienna. We are leaving. For good.

DARYL/SEREVANT *(Excitedly)*: I'll start to pack, sir.

GORDON/MESMER: You don't even know where we're going.

DARYL/SERVANT: I'm happy to go wherever you go, sir.

He exits. MESMER goes to his desk, picks up a broadsheet and
reads aloud

GORDON/MESMER: A magician of importance
    Is Mesmer, who therefore
    Can make the melancholy dance
    Without knowing why or wherefore.

Disgustedly, he throws the paper down in disgust.

GORDON/MESMER: What fools they are in Vienna. I shall go where they are willing to listen to new ideas. The capital of Europe. Paris! Where everything is possible.

HARRY plays music as MESMER exits.

HEATHER: End of Act One. Good.

GORDON: Yes, it reaches a decent climax and a sort of resolution. The trouble is, the second act has less impact. Sorry, Harry, but that's not your fault. There was just less drama about the time he spent in Paris.

HEATHER: Why do you do this, Gordon?

GORDON: What?

HEATHER: Become negative. There's a great deal of drama and conflict in the second act.

HARRY: And a few laughs.

GORDON: Sorry. It's just that I think the Maria Theresa story is the strongest event in Mesmer's life.

HARRY: Nonsense. It was only a part of a long and tempestuous journey…

GORDON: But from the audience's point of view, it's the blind pianist thing that's the most dramatic.

SANDY: Oh, give it a rest, Gordon.

GORDON: Sorry?

SANDY: You're always so defeatist. I think this is shaping up to be an excellent production, and all you do is complain and moan as usual.

GORDON: Are you getting upset because you suspect I'm right?

SANDY: I'm not getting upset. It's just that sometimes you piss me off.

GORDON: Only sometimes? Well, Sandy, you piss me off *most* of the time.

There is an embarrassed silence. GORDON has gone too far.

HEATHER: I think we ought to break for an early lunch. *(She looks at her watch)* Shall we come back at one-thirty?

DARYL: Yeah. *(To GORDON.)* And don't worry about the second act, Gordon. That French Revolution stuff's great.

GORDON has removed his rehearsal coat and starts for the exit, ignoring DARYL'S comment and shaking his head patronisingly. He stops at the exit and turns to address them all.

GORDON: Pint of Guinness and a pie is called for. Anyone care to join me at the Red Lion? Or are you all doing the health food place again?

EMMA joins him.

EMMA: I wouldn't mind giving the pub a try. You can tell me all about that TV series you did in the Eighties. *(To the others.)* I saw an episode last night on one of the satellite channels.

SANDY: You poor thing.

EMMA: It was actually quite funny.

SANDY: Unfortunately, it hasn't stood the test of time.

GORDON: How would you know?

SANDY: Because I remember it the first time around. It was dated then!

GORDON stares at SANDY with hostility.

GORDON: Enjoy your lunch! Don't choke on your nut cutlet!

He exits with EMMA

HEATHER: Oh, this is becoming so…what's wrong with the man?

SANDY: He's a bullying, self-centred piece of shit – that's what's wrong with him. And I wish to God I'd not got involved again.

HEATHER: Again?

CARL: You've worked with him before, haven't you?

SANDY: It doesn't matter. The man's a pig. Let's leave it at that.

She prepares to leave, getting her handbag from her chair.

CARL: Where was it you worked with him?

SANDY: Oh...it was a rep season...at Northampton. A long time ago.

CARL: Well, you two are going to have to call a truce.

HEATHER: For the sake of the show.

DARYL: Yeah, I've noticed you two are at each other's throats the whole time.

SANDY: Oh, let's forget it, shall we?. I'll do my best to overlook his attitude, leave him to his pie and beer and enjoy my nut cutlet. *(She laughs, having turned it into a joke.)* Anyone care to join me?

HARRY: Of course. Nut cutlets all round!

They all exit, in a more positive mood.

End of Act One.

ACT TWO

The cast return but not all at once. Some of them return while the interval is still in progress, to look at their scripts or to make a phone call or text someone on a mobile. Someone might return and then disappear again as if going to the loo. When they have all returned, with the exception of GORDON and EMMA, the house lights go down and the second act begins.

HEATHER speaks quietly to HARRY.

HEATHER: You went with Gordon to the Red Lion yesterday. How many pints did he have?

HARRY *(Reluctant to tell tales)*: Oh…um…just two or…might have been three. Can't really remember now. *(Coming to GORDON'S defence.)* But clearly it doesn't affect him. His lines are always spot on. If that was me after three pints of Guinness, I'd be slurring my words and talking gibberish.

HEATHER: He might be good on lines but –

HARRY: But what?

HEATHER: I don't know. I just get the impression that he's not giving one hundred per cent. He could be outstandingly good. Exceptional. But there always seems to be something holding him back.

HARRY: And you think it could be the booze?

HEATHER: I'm not sure.

HARRY: I wouldn't worry about it. I've seen actors like him before. Old pros. They hold back until the actual performance and then they let rip.

DARYL has wandered over and heard the last three speeches.

DARYL: Yeah. You've only got to look at musicians. Pissed *and* drugged most of the time, and *still* they manage to play their instruments. Some of them outstandingly well. If anything, I think the booze and drugs help. Fires them up. Inspires them to go beyond the ordinary and mundane.

Unnoticed, GORDON enters behind them and hears the last part of DARYL'S speech.

GORDON: Booze and drugs, eh? Anyone I know?

DARYL is embarrassed and doesn't hide it very well.

DARYL: Oh...um...we were talking about pop musicians. How they...um...still perform when they're high.

GORDON: And in what context was this observation?

DARYL: Oh...er...nothing. Just having a chat. Making conversation. Mainly about musicians.

GORDON: Mainly. But not *limited* to musicians.

CARL decides to come to DARYL'S rescue.

CARL: D'you think we ought to crack on with Act Two?

GORDON *(Ominously)*: Oh yes. Act Two.

HEATHER: We should wait for Emma.

GORDON: She's just gone to...powder her nose.

SANDY: I hope you both had a good drink.

GORDON: We did...yes...thank you. And how was your nut cutlet?

DARYL: I thought you were joking. They really did sell nut cutlets!

GORDON: Fancy that! And there we were tucking into delicious steak and kidney pies.

SANDY: Not to mention the Guinness.

GORDON: Something wrong with that? Or is it this new century political correctness gone mad? Back in the stone age everyone in the cast went to the pub at lunch time. No wonder we now have to work with rather commonplace actors.

CARL: Oh come on, Gordon – that's a bit below the belt.

GORDON *(Turning it into a joke)*: Present company excluded, dear boy.

EMMA enters.

EMMA: Sorry. I'm not late am I?

GORDON: Seeing as we wasted a whole week on warm-ups, what difference can five minutes either way make?

SANDY: Oh give it a rest, Gordon – I think the needle's stuck. We should just get on with it.

GORDON: For once, sweetheart, I concur.

SANDY looks away with disgust. EMMA turns away to get her script, and then turns back to GORDON, speaking to him but for everyone's benefit.

EMMA: Oh I meant to say, Gordon, thank you for lunch.

GORDON: You are more than welcome, my darling.

HEATHER: Okay, let's start Act Two. So that's you, Gordon, at your desk in your study in Paris. We start off with that scene about the poodle and the letter from Mesmer's wife.

GORDON/MESMER sits at the desk to write his notes. DARYL enters as the SERVANT, with a letter. HARRY plays a bit of Mozart as a curtain raiser.

DARYL/SERVANT: I went to collect the mail. There's one letter….

GORDON/MESMER: Ah! I hope it's the one I've been waiting for.

DARYL/SERVANT: It's from Vienna.

GORDON/MESMER *(Disappointed)*: Oh! My wife.

The SERVANT puts the letter on his desk, but MESMER pays it no attention and seems more interested in quizzing his SERVANT about another matter.

GORDON/MESMER: Antoine? Is that dog still outside the surgery?

DARYL/SERVANT: Six weeks he's been there. I don't know what attracts him to your surgery more than any other building in our street.

GORDON/MESMER: Have you tried to coax the poor animal inside with some food?

DARYL/SERVANT: I can't get him to come anywhere near me. It's as if he's scared of being captured.

GORDON/MESMER: But when you leave the food and come back inside, he does eat it?

DARYL/SERVANT: Oh yes. When I go out again the food is always gone. Perhaps what attracts him to your surgery is something to do with Animal Magnetism.

GORDON/MESMER: Hmm. I wonder. It's very strange. He seems to be attracted to us, yet won't come too close. And he's such a handsome poodle.

DARYL/SERVANT: Probably a stray. Why don't you try feeding him yourself, sir?

GORDON/MESMER: I tried several times when you were busy. I got the same reaction. He's showing a fear of being brought inside, and yet some force attracts him to our dwelling.

DARYL/SERVANT: As you say, it must be something to do with Animal Magnetism. I've noticed the way you talk gently to your patients. Why not try talking to the dog in the same way?

GORDON/MESMER: I have. He doesn't respond.

DARYL stops and looks towards HEATHER.

DARYL: Sorry to stop, but I had an idea. And it might get Act Two going with a big laugh. What if I reply to Gordon: 'Ask the dog how it feels, and it might answer "rough!"'

DARYL laughs at his own joke. EMMA joins in. HEATHER looks bemused, and GORDON looks disdainful.

GORDON: The old ones are the best, eh, Daryl?

DARYL: Well, I just thought....

EMMA: I thought it was quite funny.

CARL: It could work.

GORDON flashes CARL a contemptuous look.

GORDON: Oh come on, Carl. Cheap joke like that.

SANDY: I bet if it was your line, it'd be in.

GORDON: I don't think so, sweetheart.

HEATHER: We don't have to make up our minds about it now –

GORDON *(Obstinately)*: That line stays in over my dead body.

SANDY *(Sotto voce to CARL)*: In that case, let's keep it in.

GORDON *(Half turning to SANDY)*: I heard that.

> *SANDY smiles at him, and when he turns away from her she gives him the finger.*

HARRY: I think it's quite funny, Daryl, but maybe it's just...just...well...maybe it breaks up the flow. I mean, I think the audience is going to find the dog story fascinating.

DARYL: Yeah - right. We love animals in this country. Okay. It was just a thought. Sorry about that.

HEATHER: Take it from your line, Daryl: 'As you say, it must be something to do with Animal Magnetism.'

DARYL/SERVANT: As you say, it must be something to do with Animal Magnetism. I've noticed the way you talk gently to your patients. Why not try talking to the dog in the same way?

GORDON/MESMER: I have. He doesn't respond.

DARYL/SERVANT: He hangs about outside. Eats our food – at a distance. But won't befriend us. It's a mystery.

GORDON/MESMER: I would guess the dog is responding to some natural instinct. Perhaps there is a cosmic, magnetic force, pulling him towards this building. Why that is, I have no idea. It's most frustrating, wondering what to make of this creature that feels some strange energy, a compulsion to adopt my surgery as its medium, and yet it keeps its distance.

DARYL/SERVANT: Would you like me to have another go at enticing it indoors?

GORDON/MESMER: I don't think it would do any good. No. Let us forget the dog for a moment. I'd like you to run another errand for me…this one only as far as the rue d'Orsay. I want you to deliver a copy of my book on Animal Magnetism to Monsieur Deslon.

MESMER hands the servant a package.

DARYL/SERVANT: Monsieur Deslon appears to be an extremely loyal supporter.

GORDON/MESMER: One of the few. Paris is proving as bad as Vienna. It is becoming increasingly difficult to persuade members of my own fraternity, even with the incontrovertible evidence, witnessing the results with their own eyes. But don't get me started on those buffoons at the Faculty of Medicine again. As you say, at least Deslon is supportive. And I think Bergasse, too, is starting to recognise my exploration and research. At least he supports my presentation at the Faculty next month. Now please hurry along to Monsieur Deslon's. I would like to give him ample opportunity to digest the contents of my work before the presentation.

DARYL/SERVANT: Right away, sir.

GORDON/MESMER: Antoine! We have known each other long enough, and so formalities are not necessary now when we are not in company. You may call me Franz.

DARYL/SERVANT: Thank you, sir. I mean, Franz.

The SERVANT exits. MESMER stares at the letter from his wife for a moment and then reluctantly opens it and begins to read. SANDY, as his wife, enters on the opposite side of the stage to him, and she becomes the voice of his letter, but is reading from the letter she holds.

SANDY/FRAU MESMER: My Dear Franz, I know why you ran away to Paris….

GORDON/MESMER *(Angrily)*: I didn't *run away!*

SANDY/FRAU MESMER: And I do sympathise with the way you were treated in Vienna.

GORDON/MESMER: Huh!

SANDY/FRAU MESMER: I always gave you my support, both financially and with practical help at your clinic....

GORDON/MESMER: Don't make me laugh. As soon as the medical faculty turned against me, you distanced yourself from me. You didn't want to know.

SANDY/FRAU MESMER: But I realise now that we have never been close – really close. Perhaps that has something to do with our age difference. And also your obsessions.

GORDON/MESMER: Obsessions!

SANDY/FRAU MESMER: I would just like you to know that I did love you and held you in high esteem.

GORDON/MESMER: Past tense duly noted.

SANDY/FRAU MESMER: But you have made Paris your permanent home and centre of operations. And as I have no intention of abandoning my home in Austria and am ten years older than you, and neither of us are getting any younger, we may well never see one another again. I don't want us to part with bitterness, so I will bid you adieu and wish you success in your endeavours. Although I feel it my duty to remind you of that one soldier who was out of step, and thought he was the only one marching correctly. Perhaps the majority of your medical fraternity may be right. Have you ever considered that?

FRAU MESMER begins to exit.

GORDON: Just a minute! We can't both have a letter that we're reading.

SANDY: Why not?

GORDON: I would have thought it was obvious. I've received the letter and I'm reading it.

SANDY: Yes, and I'm writing it.

GORDON: Yes but it'll look ridiculous if we both have a letter. It looks far better that you look straight out front and we hear your thoughts as you compose the letter. Or were you hoping not to bother learning the lines.

SANDY: Well...I...

GORDON: Of course! You were just being lazy. Unprofessional.

SANDY: Unprofessional! Unprofessional! Hark who's bloody talking with his three pints of Guinness at lunch time.

GORDON: Two pints.

SANDY: Two pints, three pints. What's the difference?

GORDON: Knowing my limitations, that's the difference...*and* my lines!

SANDY: What do you think, Heather? You're the director.

GORDON snorts disparagingly.

HEATHER: Well, I think probably it would look better as your thoughts, but as we haven't got much rehearsal time left...

GORDON: We compromise. Huh!

SANDY *(To GORDON)*: We rehearsed this scene yesterday. Why didn't you say anything then?

GORDON: Because I thought you'd have learnt it by now. But clearly you have no intention of doing that.

CARL: Look! Can we please just get on with the rehearsal. I'm sick of this constant bickering..

HEATHER: Yes, please, Gordon, can we move on?

GORDON: Okay. *(To SANDY.)* If you can cue me in...just *read* the last line of your speech.

SANDY: Perhaps the majority of your medical fraternity may be right. Have you ever considered that?

GORDON/MESMER: How fickle could she be? Oh, yes, when I was the toast of Vienna, she believed in me, and gave me encouragement and support . But, as soon as the tide began to turn, dissatisfaction set in. She distanced herself from me. And then, when those dullards and nincompoops, who have the effrontery to call themselves scientists, made public their remonstrations against Animal Magnetism, it was as if we were no longer husband and wife. I realised long ago, that she just wanted to be the wife of a celebrity. Hypocrite!

Damn hypocrite like all the rest. *(Taking a moment's pause to calm himself.)* But at least in Paris I have many supporters, and I successfully treat the sick, both rich and poor, every day. Witnesses cannot fail to see my results and successes, and will be transformed into believers and disciples of my Animal Magnetism.

The SERVANT enters, breathlessly and excitedly.

DARYL/SERVANT: Sir! Sir! Franz!

GORDON/MESMER: What is it? Was Charles Deslon thrilled to receive my parcel?

DARYL/SERVANT: Er…yes…I gave him the parcel and he seemed pleased to receive it. But that's not why you find me in this excitable state.

GORDON/MESMER *(Smiling)*: Come on then, Antoine? Why are you so electrified?

DARYL/SERVANT: It's our canine friend. He's gone.

GORDON/MESMER: Gone?

DARYL/SERVANT: When I left here for the rue d'Orsay, the poodle followed me. It has never done that before. I kept turning round to see if it was still there, and then it would stop, as if to keep a safe distance between us. Then, as soon as I arrived at my destination, a man suddenly opened a window in the house on the opposite side of the street. He had spotted the dog and called it by name. Wagging its tail and barking excitedly, the dog ran over to him. It transpired the man had raised the dog in Moscow, and when he came to Paris just over six weeks ago, he lost him. And now they are reunited.

MESMER rises excitedly and begins pacing as he works out the reasons for this.

GORDON/MESMER: This is fascinating!. Fascinating! And it raises so many interesting questions. Did the dog choose to hang around you, Antoine, because it somehow knew you would eventually lead it to its master? Did it refuse to enter the clinic because it feared being trapped inside on the great day when you would lead it to its owner? I feel sure the animal knew what it was doing. The dog couldn't possibly be capable of logical reasoning, so it must be instinct that is the faculty operating here. Reason depends on the senses, but instinct has a direct connection with nature and therefore has certain powers denied to reason. This event was fortuitous and is a testimony to the power of Animal Magnetism. I feel inspired now. Whereas before, I felt a little wary of giving my presentation to those cretins at the Faculty, I now feel fired up with optimism.

HARRY plays a Mozart music link and CARL enters as BERGASSE, using the fourth wall as his Faculty of Medicine audience.

HEATHER: We'll record the reactions of the Faculty of Medicine attendees, but for now can we all improvise them to assist Carl and Gordon?

SANDY: Instead of recording it, why don't the rest of us do the crowd noises offstage.

HEATHER *(Gesturing out front)*: Because it's supposed to come from out there.

SANDY: In that case, why don't we go into the auditorium and become the members of the Faculty?

HEATHER: Well, there's only you, me, Harry and Daryl. And I'm guessing that the Faculty would have all been men.

She looks towards HARRY who confirms this with a nod.

SANDY: Does it matter? We're doing it in a non-realistic style. And if there's four of us, we can each take a corner of the auditorium.

HEATHER: Yes, I think it could work. But for now just do it from the wings so we can see how the lines and interruptions go.

HEATHER and HARRY stand on one side of the stage, and SANDY and CARL on the other.

HEATHER: Okay, let's take the music as read. Lots of heckling from the four of us and on you come, Carl.

As CARL does his entrance again, the four of them ad-lib lines such as 'The man is a charlatan'. 'Load of nonsense, if you ask me.' 'Come on, let's hear what he has to say.' 'We need evidence, not stupid wizardry.' 'Here comes the wizard of Vienna.' Etc., etc. CARL steps forward, raising his hands to quieten the audience.

CARL/BERGASSE: Please, gentlemen! At least give the eminent doctor an opportunity to speak. Listen to what he has to say. Don't dismiss his findings before you've had a chance to...

SANDY: He's a trickster!

DARYL: An occultist!

CARL/BERGASSE: If there was ever any truth in the rumour that he was an occultist, his doctoral degree would never – NEVER – have been approved.

HARRY: That was years ago.

HEATHER: Yes. Since then he may have studied the black arts.

General agreement from the four of them.

CARL/BERGASSE: Gentlemen, gentlemen! Order! Order! Here is Doctor Mesmer. I urge you to listen to what he has to say.

BERGASSE steps aside and MESMER moves into his space.

HARRY: My arm is broken, doctor. Can you fix it?

GORDON/MESMER: I do not heal broken bones, or prescribe remedies. The healing process is a partnership between me and my patient.

DARYL: I'll bet it is.

Dirty laughter from the rest of them.

CARL/BERGASSE: Please, gentlemen! If you will just allow Doctor Mesmer time to explain.

SANDY: I'm all ears.

HEATHER: That's hereditary. There's no cure.

More laughter. BERGASSE looks helplessly towards MESMER.

CARL/BEGASSE: Doctor?

GORDON/MESMER: I know most of you do not believe in Animal Magnetism, but I have proved beyond reasonable doubt....

HARRY: Rubbish!

GORDON/MESMER *(Heatedly)*:...proved beyond reasonable doubt that I can cure a patient by harnessing the effect of gravitation on human physiology. There is a mutual influence between heavenly bodies, the earth and living things. A universally distributed fluid, so continuous as to admit no vacuum anywhere....

DARYL: This is absolute poppycock!

HARRY: And I would like to second that!

They all start slow hand claps and chant 'Off! Off! Off!'

CARL/BERGASSE *(To Mesmer)*: Cut to the demonstration?

MESMER nods his agreement and goes off to fetch EMMA/ODETTE. BERGASSE raises his hands to silence the crowd who eventually quieten down, especially as they see ODETTE being helped into a chair by MESMER, and she shakes uncontrollably, as if she has Parkinson's Disease.

CARL/BERGASSE: This is Odette who has fits and cannot stop shaking. I believe some of you physicians have attempted to treat her and have failed. Now let us see what Doctor Mesmer can do for Odette.

MESMER sits opposite ODETTE – they are both profile to the audience – and their knees are touching. He begins to soothe her by running his arms along her arms and stroking her shoulders and face.

GORDON/MESMER: Odette, I want you to relax and trust me. The magnetic fluid will pass from my body into yours, and it will make you feel better. Look into my eyes and feel yourself drifting into a soothing sensation of well-being.

She begins to relax and the shaking becomes less violent, just the occasional twitch.

GORDON/MESMER: That's good. You are starting to feel so much better and more relaxed.

SANDY: All that caressing. I expect he feels better, too.

Sniggers from the crowd. MESMER glares angrily at SANDY and rises to fetch his wand. He waves the wand a little distance away from ODETTE, and every so often moves closer to her and rubs it against her arms and the side of her head, moving about like a stage conjuror. ODETTE relaxes completely.

GORDON/MESMER: How do you feel now, Odette.

EMMA/ODETTE: I can't believe how relaxed I feel. So calm. And all the shaking has ended.

GORDON/MESMER *(Addressed partly to the audience)*: And that's after only one session. A few more sessions and she should be permanently cured.

HEATHER: This proves nothing. She could have been faking it.

DARYL: I bet he put her up to this.

SANDY: I said he was a trickster.

HARRY: The man's a fraud. I can't stay here a moment longer.

DARYL: And I have better things to do with my time.

CARL/BERGASSE: Stay, gentlemen. How can you ignore the heavenly harmony we have witnessed here today? *(To MESMER.)* They've gone. All gone. I'm sorry, Franz, they were biased right from the start.

GORDON/MESMER: Those ignorant fools! Like those bigots who refused to look through Galileo's telescope.

CARL/BERGASSE: And if ever proof were needed…Odette has experienced a positive transformation.

EMMA/ODETTE: Thank you, Doctor Mesmer. I will be forever in your debt. But you mentioned further treatment….

GORDON/MESMER: Perhaps two more sessions. But don't look so worried. As a cook, you perform a valuable role in society, as so many others do, yet your recompense is small, compared to the privileged classes. There will be no charge for your treatment.

EMMA/ODETTE: Thank you, doctor.

GORDON/MESMER: You may go now, Odette. And I will see you at the same time next week at my surgery.

ODETTE exits.

GORDON/MESMER: Thank you for being a loyal supporter. You realise this endangers your standing at the Faculty, don't you?

CARL/BERGASSE: I don't care. I believe in Animal Magnetism.

GORDON/MESMER: But without the backing of the scientific institutes in Paris, things will be difficult. Look at what has happened to Charles Deslon. He is most influential as private physician to Louis XVl's brother, and still the Faculty have suspended his voting rights for one year because he supports Animal Magnetism.

CARL/BERGASSE: A pox on the institutes! Why not petition the king for support?

GORDON/MESMER: The king doesn't want to know. Which is why I have petitioned Marie Antoinette, instead.

CARL/BERGASSE: And?

GORDON/MESMER: Her mother died recently, and she remains in mourning in Versailles. But she has agreed for the Comte de Maurepas, the Minister of State, to act in her name. Charles Deslon and I are meeting him next week.

CARL/BERGASSE: Good. I hope we can count on their financial assistance so that we can spread the influence of Mesmerism throughout France.

GORDON/MESMER: Is that what they are calling it now? Mesmerism?

CARL/BERGASSE: Your fame is spreading. And speaking of fame: have you heard that Mozart and Maria Theresa Paradies are in Paris?

GORDON/MESMER: Yes, I had heard. No doubt Maria's loathsome parents will be accompanying her.

CARL/BERGASSE: You once told me you thought they were responsible for her blindness. But they dote on her. Surely you still don't subscribe to the view....

GORDON/MESMER: I have little doubt they were to blame. I saw with my own eyes the abuse and the bullying.

CARL/BERGASSE: And yet, she is one of the greatest pianists the world has known.

GORDON/MESMER: Yes, I wish I could hear her play once more. But I find it necessary to avoid her parents at all costs.

CARL/BERGASSE: You're not frightened of them, are you?

GORDON/MESMER: On the contrary. I fear for my own conduct if I should confront them. An altercation at the theatre would give my enemies further cause for resentment.

CARL/BERGASSE: But you would still like to see Maria Theresa perform?

GORDON/MESMER: I hunger and thirst for her sweet music.

CARL/BERGASSE: Then why not join me in my box at the theatre?

GORDON/MESMER: Yes but....

CARL/BERGASSE: You can arrive at the very last minute, and sneak into my box, incognito, as it were.

GORDON/MESMER: I should be delighted to accept your offer.*(Shaking BERGASSE'S hand.)* Thank you, my dear friend.

BERGASSE turns to exit. MESMER calls after him.

GORDON/MESMER: What will Maria be performing? Do you know?

CARL/BERGASSE: The Concerto in B Flat Major.

BERGASSE exits. HARRY clicks on the CD player which plays Mozart's Concerto in B Flat Major, while DARYL and SANDY set MESMER'S table/desk.

While they do this, MESMER stands listening to the concerto, as it fades out he speaks before crossing to his desk.

GORDON/MESMER *(Applauding)*: Bravo, Maria! Bravo! An exquisite concert. Perhaps I was wrong to bring you out of darkness. Perhaps you are happier in the brilliance of your music.

He crosses and sits at his desk and finishes writing a letter. The SERVANT enters.

DARYL/SERVANT: You wanted to see me, Franz.

GORDON/MESMER: Yes. I have a letter I want sent to the Palace of Versailles.

CARL/SERVANT: How did your meeting with the Minister of State go?

GORDON/MESMER: Badly, Antoine. Although he is authorised by the king and queen to provide me with a generous pension to start my school of Animal Magnetism, he said I would be required to accept a number of pupils named by the government. No doubt these pupils will report to the authorities on what I'm doing.

DARYL/SERVANT: And so you turned it down.

GORDON/MESMER: Of course. All I have ever wanted is official recognition of Animal Magnetism. So now I'm writing to the queen to ask for the conditions to be lifted. *(Arrogantly.)* I've told her that if my valuable work isn't recognized then I will be forced to seek new pastures, which may provoke cries of despair from the sick and suffering of Paris. *(Seeing an expression of doubt on ANTOINE'S face.)* What's wrong?

DARYL/SERVANT: If you don't mind my saying, that sounds like blackmail.

GORDON/MESMER: I don't care, Antoine. There is much discontent among the poor. I would applaud the rising of the people in the name of a more egalitarian society. Which reminds me, I have to visit a poor washerwoman who suffers from epileptic fits, and I'm already running late. Please send the letter for me.

MESMER exits. The SERVANT picks up the letter and addresses the audience.

DARYL/SERVANT: I sent the letter to the queen, and my master waited weeks for a reply. None came. But Franz didn't carry out his idle threat and abandon the poor of Paris. Instead, along with many of his disciples and devotees, such as Bergasse and Deslon, he founded *(like a TV presenter's announcement)* THE SOCIETY OF HARMONY!

He exits. Enter CARL/BERGASSE.

CARL/BERGASSE *(To audience)*: From time to time I was plunged into a clinical depression from which I was rescued by Dr Mesmer. I became a true believer in Animal Magnetism, as did Charles Deslon. The Society of Harmony was formed and all over France new clinics opened, sponsored by many rich clients, such as Princess de Lamballe.

By way of introduction, he turns to SANDY/PRINCESS as she enters.

SANDY/PRINCESS: While Dr Mesmer did not exactly cause my ulcer to disappear, he did provide sufficient relief for me to persuade my husband to become a sponsor. Although, over the years, I found it difficult to ignore the constant vitriol of the press.

HARRY enters as a newspaper reporter, carrying a quill pen and reporter's notebook.

HARRY/REPORTER: Our readers should ask themselves whether this Society of Harmony consists of secret lodges attempting to compete with Freemasonry. And, worse still, is Doctor Mesmer another Casanova?

CARL/BERGASSE: The press surely cannot ignore the influence of Mesmerian culture on the French population.

HARRY/REPORTER: It is an epidemic, infecting France like a disease. We condemn Mesmerism on the grounds of morality. I went undercover to an Animal Magnetism clinic in Lyons, and saw with my own eyes female patients being treated by male magnetizers. I made an excuse and left!

CARL/BERGASSE: Mesmerism treats every patient with true equality, and we in the Society of Harmony now strongly believe in political freedom. Political Mesmerians should make a clean sweep of the unnatural institutions of France, including the absolute monarchy.

SANDY/PRINCESS: But they have no qualms about accepting our money, yet they bite the hand that feeds them. And they accuse us of hypocrisy!

CARL/BERGASSE: Long live Mesmerism.

SANDY/PRINCESS: Long live the ruling class.

HARRY/REPORTER: And long live France. *(With a chuckle.)* Whoever butters our bread!

They exit. HEATHER plays a music link as MESMER enters and sits at his desk reading a newspaper. He throws it down in disgust and rises.

GORDON/MESMER: Still I get a barrage of hatred from the establishment. Will this tide of trash never cease. Huh! Just you wait all you doubters, come the revolution!

DARYL enters hurriedly.

DARYL/SERVANT: Franz! We must close all the shutters and put up barricades. The Bastille has been stormed, the political prisoners released and the people are rioting. The revolution has begun!

GORDON/MESMER *(Aside)*: I spoke too soon!

HEATHER: And that's a fast blackout, music link, and straight into the next scene.

HARRY operates the music, while MESMER sits at his desk

HEATHER: Lights up.

The SERVANT enters.

GORDON/MESMER: What news, Antoine?

DARYL/SERVANT: Not good I fear. The Reign of Terror has truly begun. Following her husband to the guillotine, the queen has now been beheaded. And every day, hundreds are drawn by tumbrel to that bloodthirsty blade, while the crowds scream with delight, and flock to the square to watch the event, like hungry predators devouring their prey. It's obscene.

GORDON/MESMER: But who can really blame the people of Paris? Having suffered the degradations of poverty for so long, and seen the obscene life-style of the aristocracy, they are understandably angry. But there are also many innocent people being condemned to death.

DARYL/SERVANT: And what about your position, Franz? How have you managed to keep your head well below the parapet?

GORDON/MESMER: That's the point, Antoine: I haven't. Long before the revolution began, I spoke out for the people, saw the injustice and social inequality that was damaging this nation. That hasn't gone unnoticed with the revolutionary committee. And I have always treated the poor with respect and never charged them for my services.

DARYL/SERVANT: All the same, the committee sometimes make grotesque decisions when choosing their next victims.

GORDON/MESMER: Trust me, Antoine. We are safe. Believe me…we are safe.

CARL, who as risen from his side of stage chair to get up for his entrance, knocks on an imaginary door. Scared, ANTOINE freezes.

GORDON/MESMER: Well, go on, answer it.

The SERVANT goes upstage and returns with CARL/ROBESPIERRE moments later.

DARYL/SERVANT: His honour, Monsieur Robespierre.

ROBESPIERRE moves down to shake hands with MESMER. He avoids looking him in the eye.

GORDON/MESMER: Welcome, Monsieur Robespierre. *(To the SERVANT.)* Please leave us.

ROBESPIERRE looks around and up at the ceiling, as if he is surveying a fine apartment.

CARL/ROBESPIERRE: You seem to live in great style, Herr Mesmer.

GORDON/MESMER: This is also my surgery, where anyone –
even the poorest of the poor- may be treated gratis.

CARL/ROBESPIERRE *(Impatiently, waving it aside)*: Yes, yes! I
know of your background, and how you have treated the
working classes with missionary zeal. But rather than send
one of my agents to see you, I thought I would visit you
myself, and observe first hand your fine living. *(MESMER
goes to object and ROBESPIERRE silences him with a raised
hand.)* But mainly to hear your pleas on behalf of Bergasse.
It is well known that you no longer speak to each other.

GORDON/MESMER: We fell out many years ago. But that is no
reason to want to see him dead. And he's a loyal
revolutionary.

CARL/ROBESPIERRE: It will be up to the Tribunal to decide.
But I will put in a word for you.

GORDON/MESMER; Thank you. Do you mind if I ask you
something, Monsieur Robespierre? *(ROBESPIERRE looks at
him for the first time, waiting for him to continue.)* Bergasse
was a far more outspoken supporter of the revolution than I
was, yet he is under threat of execution and I remain free of
intimidation.

CARL/ROBESPIERRE: You are a foreign national, Herr Mesmer

GORDON/MESMER: So was Marie Antionette.

CARL/ROBESPIERRE: She became queen of our country and
ruled with an indifference for the people's needs. Her
flippant remark about letting them eat cake, for a start....

GORDON/MESMER: I can't believe she really said that. Not when
she did. It sounds like revolutionary propaganda.

*ROBESPIERRE stares at MESMER as though he has
overstepped the mark.*

CARL/ROBESPIERRE: In spite of all your work treating the poor,
you remain a considerably rich man. And so you will forfeit
eighty per cent of your wealth and your property will be
requisitioned.

GORDON/MESMER: But my surgery....

CARL/ROBESPIERRE: An unnecessary luxury. Less ostentatious premises will do just as well. I will send my auditors around to make an assessment. *(He goes to exit and then turns back.)* Why *are* you pleading for Bergasse's life, seeing as you have fallen out?

GORDON/MESMER: I am a doctor and scientist, having devoted my life to healing. I cannot condone capital punishment, even though I do not support the aristocracy and greedy minority.

CARL/ROBESPIERRE: The national razor will trim the population of that vermin.

GORDON/MESMER: The ills in society cannot be repaired by mass executions.

CARL/ROBESPIERRE: To punish the oppressors of humanity is clemency; to forgive is barbarity.

ROBESPIERRE exits.

GORDON/MESMER: Reign of Terror sound bite! I wonder who wrote it for him?

The SERVANT enters.

DARYL/SERVANT: How did the meeting with that architect of misery go?

GORDON dashes across to his chair, fetches his script, turns to the appropriate page, and returns, reading from the script.

GORDON/MESMER: My life is secure, but my capital and property are drastically diminished. And while Paris wallows in an orgy of bloodshed, I think we ought to seek a more salubrious city.

SANDY: Is Mesmer reading that from a letter?

GORDON: Sorry? Are you in this scene?

SANDY: Oh, it's all right for *him* to read from the script, but when I...

GORDON: I'm reading from the script because there is only one more scene to go, and I will know it by tomorrow. So please keep your bloody comments to yourself.

CARL: These interruptions are ruining the rehearsal.

GORDON: Blame her for this one.

SANDY: Oh, yes, you've always got to have someone to blame – someone to pick on. I should never have got involved with you again.

CARL: Is this what it was like when you worked together in rep?

DARYL: Northampton, wasn't it?

GORDON: Is that what she told you?

HEATHER: She said you were at Northampton rep together years ago.

GORDON: We've never worked together *(To SANDY.)* Why did you lie? Wishful thinking was it?

SANDY: Far from it. They guessed I'd known you in the past, and I just couldn't bring myself to tell them.

GORDON: About our blissful marriage.

EMMA: Marriage! You were married?

GORDON: Oh yes, two years of sheer misery.

SANDY: I second that. I've never lived with such a lazy bastard in all my life.

GORDON: Oh, don't start that feminist bullshit. Complaints about leaving the toilet seat up?

SANDY: If only it was the seat. I had to mop up the puddles on the toilet floor when you were in your cups.

GORDON: What women never understand is that one small hair in the barrel can deflect one's aim.

SANDY: You see why it only lasted two years.

GORDON: And you did all right out of it. She got the proceeds from the sale of the house. A house that was paid for by my telly series from long before I knew her. No wonder I never married again. I realised I could find someone I didn't like very much and buy them a house instead.

CARL *(To SANDY)*: So why did you agree to do this show knowing he'd be in it?

SANDY: I hoped time would have done it's healing.

CARL: Well it hasn't, and we're all on the receiving end of your arguments.

HEATHER: Yes, why can't you put your differences aside, and both behave like professionals?

GORDON and SANDY glare at her. HARRY, suddenly taking on the role of arbitrator, steps forward.

HARRY: As far as I can see, you are both going to be excellent in this production, so why not respect each other as performers, even though you might have personal differences? I'm sure you are both rational enough to set aside those disagreements and behave in a businesslike fashion.

GORDON: You're right, Harry. Sorry, everyone. Sandy.

SANDY: I'm happy to let bygones...

HEATHER: Good. Now where were we?

GORDON/MESMER: I'll give you the cue, Daryl. And while Paris wallows in an orgy of bloodshed, I think we ought to seek a more salubrious city.

DARYL/SERVANT: London?

GORDON/MESMER: Vienna.

DARYL/SERVANT: But relations between France and Austria are not good. They talk of war.

GORDON/MESMER: What has that to do with me? Austria is my homeland. While they may not welcome me back like the prodigal son, I don't expect any trouble there. Start packing. I have one more surgery to attend to.

Music link as MESMER and the SERVANT exit. CARL enters as an AUSTRIAN OFFICIAL, and he sits behind a desk. From the side of the stage HARRY makes an announcement.

HARRY: Her Highness, Princess Gonzaga!

EMMA enters as the PRINCESS and THE OFFICIAL stands, bows and gestures for her to take a seat. Once they are both seated, THE OFFICIAL smiles at her before speaking.

CARL/OFFICIAL 1: Your highness, you wished to see me on an important matter. A matter of state security, I believe.

EMMA/GONZAGA: Yes, I shall get straight to the point. It's about Doctor Mesmer.

CARL/OFFICIAL 1: Ah yes: I heard he was back in Vienna.

EMMA/GONZAGA: Bringing his radical views with him. A spy for the French revolution, I shouldn't wonder.

CARL/OFFCIAL 1: You have evidence of this?

EMMA/GORGANZA: I have witnesses to the heated argument I had with him.

CARL/OFFICIAL 1: What about?

EMMA/GORGANZA: He supported the revolution and the terrible regicides happening in France.

CARL/OFFICIAL 1: This is very serious. Treasonable.

EMMA/GORGANZA: I thought you ought to know.

CARL/OFFICIAL 1: Thank you for bringing it to our attention. It will be investigated immediately.

EMMA/GORGANZA: Thank you, sir.

He rises as she exits. He and HARRY move the table and place a chair centre stage, facing front. Music link, dramatic piece by Beethoven (at this period of history, Mozart was dead and Beethoven had moved to Vienna). DARYL, wearing a different rehearsal costume – something a jailer might wear, and carrying a large bunch of keys, brings on MESMER, and sits him roughly in the chair centre stage. He exits. MESMER sits staring out front, looking dejected and miserable. Enter OFFICIAL 1 and OFFICIAL 2 (HARRY), who are his interrogators. They stand either side of him, and move around as they do a good cop, bad cop routine.

HARRY/OFFICIAL 2: You deny being a dangerous radical, yet you support the wild men of the Seine, who murdered their king and established an insane republic.

GORON/MESMER: Two months you've kept me locked up and you ask me the same questions over and over. I agree I am a radical, believing in an overhaul of the political system for a fairer and more just society. But I do not condone bloodshed.

CARL/OFFICIAL 1: Yet you support those monsters who killed our late Empress's daughter. You ought to be hanged. Even the guillotine is too humane an end for the likes of you.

HARRY/OFFICIAL 2: Sadly, this is the Age of Reason. Tell us why you met with that monster Robespierre.

GORDON/MESMER: I've told you.

CARL/OFFICIAL 1: Again!

GORDON/MESMER: To plead clemency for an old colleague.

CARL/OFFICIAL 1: And this colleague – what happened?

GORDON/MESMER: I believe he escaped that humane instrument of death.

CARL/OFFICIAL 1: Thus proving you collaborated with that bloodthirsty enemy of decency and his Reign of Terror. You should be taken to the Vienna Woods to be hanged from a nearby tree.

HARRY/OFFICIAL 2: Sadly, this is the Age of Reason. Why did your secret society support the early revolution and political reforms?

GORDON/MESMER: Because we didn't think it would lead to bloodshed. We were moderate. We wanted economic change. A better life for everyone.

CARL/OFFICIAL 1: As you were a secret society, we only have your word for that. Are you here to spy for the revolutionaries?

GORDON/MESMER: No, I came here to escape the revolution.

HARRY/OFFICIAL 2: Princess Gorganza told us you found it difficult to differentiate between the excesses of the Jacobins and the justified struggle for freedom under the Gerondins.

GORDON/MESMER: It was a cerebral argument.

CARL/OFFICIAL 1: Know what I think? I think you're a dirty, sneaky spy for the French riff-raff. A fifth columnist and enemy of the state.

GORDON/MESMER: I've done nothing but hold political opinions. Unless you wish to charge me for thought crimes.

CARL/OFFICIAL 1: That may happen, not in my lifetime, but it will come. And even though I've been unable to find enough evidence to hang you, if it were up to me, I should string you up myself and let the rooks feed off you.

He walks a little away from MESMER and whispers confidentially to his colleague.

After a moment he returns to MESMER.

CARL/OFFICIAL 1: We have a dossier on you which is almost a thousand pages long, yet we can find no evidence of any serious crime being committed. You are free to go. However, we now consider you as *persona non grata* in Vienna and advise you to get out of town as soon as possible. Have you anything to say before we release you?

GORDON/MESMER *(Rises)*: Yes. Clearly we live in the Age of Reason.

CARL/OFFICIAL 1: Go tell that to the French!

The actors grind to a halt, step out of character, and GORDON gestures helplessly towards HARRY.

GORDON: So now what?

HARRY: After the Reign of Terror had ended, Mesmer returned to Paris, and now, while Napoleon Bonaparte was the man of the hour, Mesmer successfully sued the authorities for his financial losses.

GORDON: I'm not talking about a history lesson, Harry. We don't have an ending for the play, for God's sakes.

HARRY: I promise you, Gordon – everyone – if it takes me all night to write the last two scenes, you will have them by email first thing tomorrow.

GORDON: But today's Friday. We open on Thursday, need to do a technical and a dress rehearsal on Wednesday, so that gives us only two more days rehearsal. Know what I think. I think we have to rehearse all weekend.

HEATHER: We can't, Gordon. We've all got family commitments.

GORDON: Bugger the family commitments!

HEATHER: I've got my sister's wedding this weekend.

GORDON: And bugger your sister's wedding!

HEATHER: Gordon, there's no call for that....

GORDON *(To HARRY)*: So how does this play actually end then?

HARRY *(Uncertainly)*: Well, he became reclusive, moved to Switzerland and became a forgotten man until his death in 1815.

GORDON: Oh, great. What a dramatic ending. This play has to be completely restructured, you know that.

HARRY: What!

GORDON: It could start with his death, and the whole play would be a flashback of his life, and the climax in the second act must be the story about the blind girl. That's the climax. The icing on the cake. And you all know I'm right. What about you, Emma? You know I'm right, don't you?

EMMA: Well, yes, as a matter of fact....

HEATHER: We don't have the time to make those major changes, Gordon.

GORDON: And why is that, sweetheart? I'll tell you why. Because you spent a whole week buggering about with stupid games. If we hadn't done that, we'd now have at least four days to sort this out.

SANDY: See how he likes to bully people.

GORDON: Well, it's all her bloody fault. *(To HEATHER.)* Yes, you and you alone. So I say we've got to abandon family commitments and work over the weekend. Otherwise this play's had it.

HEATHER: I can't do that, Gordon. It's my sister's wedding for God's sake.

DARYL: I could rehearse Sunday morning.

GORDON: Oh shut the up, Daryl!

CARL: No, you shut it, Gordon. You pompous clown.

GORDON: What did you say?

SANDY: Spot on. I'd say it was a perfect description.

GORDON: This is because deep down, you know I'm right about this. Well, you've had your last chance. Bollocks to you all. I'm walking.

CARL: What! You can't do that.

GORDON: Watch me.

SANDY: You selfish bastard. Leaving everyone high and dry.

GORDON: I'm leaving the acting profession. I've had enough. Time to hang up my histrionics..

SANDY: He won't give up the business. What else would he do?

GORDON: Teach English to foreign students. It suddenly starts to look attractive. Regular salary and all that. And I'll tell you something: last night, when I thought about a career change, I started to feel guilty about leaving you in the lurch. But after today, I don't. Bollocks to you all, I say. Bollocks, bollocks, bollocks! I am off. *(To EMMA.)* I don't suppose you want that lift home now?

EMMA: Well, not if you're...

GORDON: Giving up the business? No. Wouldn't be much use to you now, would I? All that pathetic, it's who you know in this business. What a load of bollocks. Goodbye!

He storms off. A pause. The others are shocked and stunned.

DARYL *(Thoughtfully)*: I suppose he'll end up like Mesmer – a forgotten man. Life imitates art.

HEATHER: Now what do we do?

HARRY: We'll have to cancel. Who's going to phone the venues?

EMMA *(Starts crying)*: Oh, why did he have to...I was so looking forward to...and he promised me...

DARYL: What?

EMMA: It doesn't matter.

SANDY goes to her and puts an arm round her.

SANDY: He does that to everyone, Emma. We'll just have to manage without him. Carry on.

HEATHER: How? We've lost the leading character. Will someone please tell me how we can continue?

CARL gets an idea and clicks his fingers.

CARL: Hey! Daryl's given me an idea.

DARYL: Have I?

CARL: Life imitates art, you said. *(To HEATHER.)* What was it you said just before Gordon arrived this morning? We can improvise what you said from memory.

HEATHER: I'm not with you.

CARL: You asked where he was, if anyone had tried his mobile. Just say that and cue me in.

HEATHER: I still don't...

CARL: Go on, just say that prior to my entrance. *(CARL exits.)*

HEATHER: Where on earth is Gordon? Has anyone tried his mobile?

CARL enters, doing a very good impression of GORDON.

CARL: Morning, everyone. So, so sorry. The traffic was unbloody-believable. I do apologise. The only thing that kept me from having a coronary due to stress was the realisation that I'm not in the first scene.

EMMA: Oh, I get it!

DARYL: Life imitating art. Or vice versa now.

CARL *(To HARRY)*: Might just work, Harry. What do you think?

HARRY smiles, presses the play on the CD player, and a rousing part of Beethoven's 9th Symphony blasts out.

No one is really sure what HARRY thinks.

Curtain.

Lightning Source UK Ltd.
Milton Keynes UK
UKHW022133180619
344628UK00015B/233/P